Celebra Jesus

MW00855724

A Child's Book of the Sacraments

**You are invited to explore
seven celebrations of faith... and more!**

Who: _____
(Your name)

Hosted by: Jesus and your faith community

RSVP: Don't delay, respond today!
Just turn the page...

Pflaum Publishing Group
Dayton, OH
Milwaukee, WI

A note to parents and catechists

Faith is a wonderful gift to share with the children in your care. Representing the Church, we teach them our beliefs and we tell them our stories. But behind our words are profound experiences of God's love. We celebrate these experiences in the sacraments.

This book will introduce your children to the sacraments. It will connect each celebration to a story about Jesus. It will identify the rituals and their symbols. And it will invite your children to receive the grace that is always available. Now, that's something to celebrate!

Text and activities by Jean Buell

First and foremost, Jean is a parent who wants her home to be a place of faith, hope, and love. She has facilitated many worship and learning experiences for children and families. Other titles in this popular series by Jean include *Welcome Children! A Child's Mass Book; Sacred Stories: A Child's Bible Book; God's Heroes: A Child's Book of Saints;* and *Pray With Mary: A Child's Book of the Rosary.* All are available from Pflaum Publishing Group.

Cover illustrations: Elizabeth Swisher
Interior design: Jean Buell and Ellen Wright
Editor: Jean Larkin

Nihil obstat: Reverend Tom Knoebel, March 27, 2007
Imprimatur: †Most Reverend Timothy M. Dolan, Archbishop of Milwaukee, March 30, 2007

Pflaum Publishing Group
2621 Dryden Road, Suite 300
Dayton, OH 45439
800-543-4383
www.pflaum.com

ISBN 978-1-933178-67-7

Celebrate With Jesus

Welcome!

Do you like celebrations? Most people do. If you like celebrations, take a big breath and say, "YES!!!"

What is your favorite celebration?

_____

When does this celebration take place?

_____

What are some highlights of this celebration?

- _____

- _____

- _____

Celebrations are joyful times. We gather with family and friends. We honor special people. And we remember special events. The festivities show us the goodness of life!

Look at these pictures. Which celebrations can you name? Now look at a calendar. Which celebrations are coming soon?

Celebrate With Jesus

Many celebrations take place over and over. They are called traditions. These "back-words" will tell you more about them. Write them forwards. Look back on the traditions you know. Look ahead to new ones, too!

SEIROTS __ __ __ __ __ __ __ are the words. They tell about the people we honor and the events we remember. Sometimes, we hear the same stories over and over. That's okay. That's how we remember them!

SLAUTIR __ __ __ __ __ __ __ are the actions. They help us learn the stories. And they give us something to do! They involve our senses—touching, hearing, seeing, tasting, and smelling.

SLOBMYS __ __ __ __ __ __ __ are objects with special meanings. We know the meanings deep in our hearts.

ELPOEP __ __ __ __ __ __ are the persons who celebrate together. We share the same stories, rituals, and symbols. We feel connected to one another.

STFIG __ __ __ __ __ are the surprise packages. We don't know what's inside until we open them. But we do know this—they represent love. Love is invisible. And it doesn't always come in packages!

When we celebrate with Jesus, we honor and remember something very special— God's love. These celebrations are called "sacraments." Look back—they are traditions of our faith. Look ahead— they are for you!

Try this: Take a deep breath. Blow it into the palm of your hand. Your breath is invisible, right? Now put a tissue in your palm. Take a deep breath and blow again. How do you know your breath is there? The tissue gives you a "visible sign."

Visible signs help us notice invisible things—like God's love. Daily life is full of visible signs. Imagine seeing a bright rainbow or feeling a tight hug. Something stirs inside our hearts. We notice God's love *around* us. And we feel joy. These are sacred moments!

The sacraments are full of visible signs, too. Imagine seeing the flicker of a candle—or feeling a tickle of holy water. Something stirs inside our hearts. We notice God's love *within* us. And we feel joy. These are sacred moments, too!

The sacraments are full of sacred moments. Here's how you can remember:

SACRED + A + MOMENTS

SACRAMENTS

When we celebrate with Jesus, we celebrate many sacred moments. The more we celebrate, the more we will notice. And the more we notice, the more we will experience God's love! That is how we grow in faith.

And now... Jesus invites you to celebrate with him. Are you ready? If you are, take one more big breath and say, "YES!!!"

Turn the page to explore some more.

Celebrate With Jesus

Baptism—the Beginning

Jesus celebrated Baptism. It was the beginning of his mission.

One day, Jesus went to the Jordan River. That's where his cousin John baptized many people. John was surprised to see Jesus! John did not feel worthy to baptize Jesus. But Jesus told him to go ahead. So Jesus stepped into the river, and John baptized him.

When Jesus came out of the water, amazing things happened! The Holy Spirit came to him. And a voice came out of the sky. The voice said, "This is my beloved son. I am very pleased with him." (See Matthew 3:13-17.)

When we celebrate Baptism, we celebrate with Jesus. It is a beginning for us, too. We begin to follow Jesus. We join his Church. And we share his mission.

Either a priest or a deacon may baptize. Here are some highlights from our baptismal celebration.
- We listen to sacred stories from the Bible.
- We remember God's promise to love us. We promise to love God, too. The parents and godparents promise to help the ones being baptized grow in faith.
- The priest or deacon uses holy water to bless the ones being baptized. He says, "I baptize you in the name of the Father, and of the Son, and of the Holy Spirit." Then he anoints them with the oil of chrism. They are now baptized.
- The newly baptized persons wear white clothing.
- The priest or deacon gives them a candle. Its flame comes from the Easter candle— also called the paschal candle.
- We welcome the newly baptized persons into our faith community.

At Baptism, we are blessed with holy water. It comes from a big basin called a "baptismal font." Water is a symbol. It helps us remember God's goodness. Water is needed for life. How many ways have you used water today?

Look at the top of this baptismal font. Draw your reflection in the water. Then start at the arrow. Write every other letter in the blanks below. What is the special message for you?

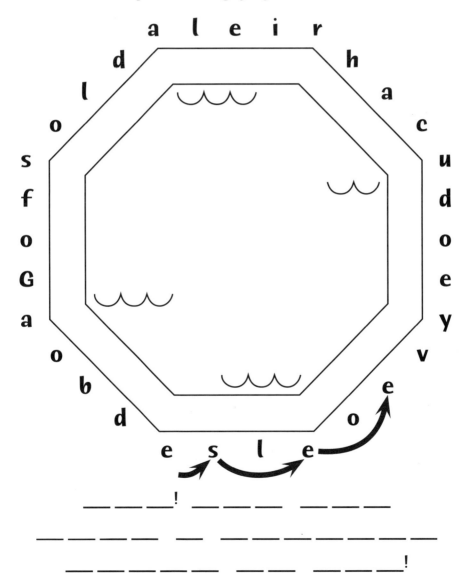

__ __ __ __ ! __ __ __ __ __ __

__ __ __ __ __ __ __ __ __ __ __ __

__ __ __ __ __ __ __ __ __ __ !

Celebrate With Jesus

We are all children of God. Imagine what that means! God's love wraps around us like a great big hug. Deep inside the wrapping is a special gift from God.

God's gift is like the word below—we don't see it, but we know it's there. What is this gift called? Lay a pencil along the dotted lines. Now you can see it!

At Baptism, this invisible gift is "opened" within us. It is God's divine life and goodness. It is friendship with Jesus. And it is partnership with the Holy Spirit. Now, that's something to celebrate!

But that's not all—this gift will grow! It will grow in all the sacred moments of our lives. And it will grow whenever we celebrate with Jesus. Baptism is just the beginning!

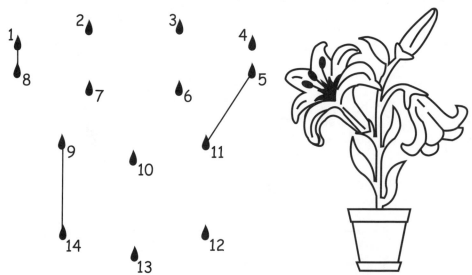

Connect the "drops" to make a baptismal font.

When we celebrate Baptism, we use the Easter, or paschal, candle. It reminds us of Jesus, who said, "I am the Light of the World." When the priest or deacon gives us a small candle lit from the Easter candle, we receive a tiny spark of Jesus' light.

When you pray today, imagine your tiny spark. Listen for Jesus. What do you hear? Follow the code to find a message.

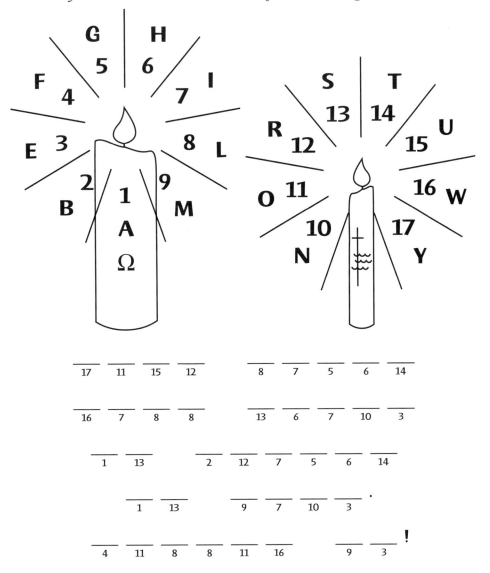

17 11 15 12   8 7 5 6 14

16 7 8 8   13 6 7 10 3

1 13   2 12 7 5 6 14

1 13   9 7 10 3 .

4 11 8 8 11 16   9 3 !

Baptism begins our adventure of faith.

Celebrate With Jesus

Confirmation—a Commitment

Jesus knew God's love. He promised to love God, too. That was his commitment. The Holy Spirit gave Jesus the power to love and serve the people.

After the resurrection, Jesus made a promise to his followers. He told them to wait in Jerusalem. "Very soon," he said, "you will be baptized by the Holy Spirit. And you will receive special power." Then Jesus returned to heaven.

The disciples waited together. It was the day of Pentecost. Suddenly, they heard the sound of a strong wind. Then a tongue of fire appeared above each person's head. They were filled with the Holy Spirit. They went out and spoke to others as the Holy Spirit directed them. (See Acts 1:4-8; 2:1-4.)

When we celebrate Confirmation, we celebrate with Jesus. We celebrate our commitment to love and follow him. The Holy Spirit will help us love and serve the people around us.

The bishop of our diocese confirms us. Here are some highlights of our celebration.
* We listen to sacred stories from the Bible.
* We renew our baptismal promises to love God.
* The bishop prays for the candidates. He lays his hands on their heads. If there are many candidates, he may extend his hands to include all the candidates.
* The bishop anoints the candidates with the oil of chrism. He says, "Be sealed by the Holy Spirit."
* The bishop sends the candidates forth. He says, "Peace be with you."
* We celebrate Eucharist, if our Confirmation is during a Mass.

At Confirmation, the bishop welcomes us. He prays with us. He places his hands on our heads. And he anoints us with oil. These are ancient traditions. They connect us to Jesus and to all of his followers. We belong to a BIG Church!

Look at these pictures. Say them out loud. Listen carefully. Then write the words on the lines below.

U　　　　**R**　　　 **+ ed**

_____　　_____　　_____.

 **– mb**　　 **– f**　**S +**  **+ it**

_____　　_____　　_____

　　ins +  **+ R**　　**U**

_____　　_____

 **– c**　　**3 – r**　　**N + R + G**

_____　　_____

 **– d**　　

_____　　_____.

11

Celebrate With Jesus

The Holy Spirit inspires us. Imagine what that means! When we are ready, change will happen. We will ask new questions. We will make new choices. We will discover new ways to love God and one another.

The Holy Spirit's gift is like the word below—we don't see it, but we know it's there. What is this gift called? Lay a pencil along the dotted lines. Now you can see it!

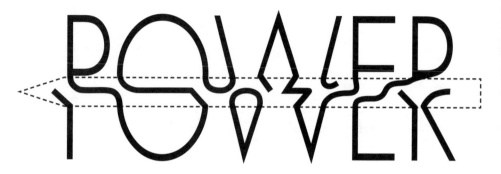

This gift is the energy that creates the change. It isn't magic. It isn't forcefulness. It is love! It is God's way of helping us become the best we can be. It leads to these:

Fruits of the Holy Spirit   Gifts of the Holy Spirit

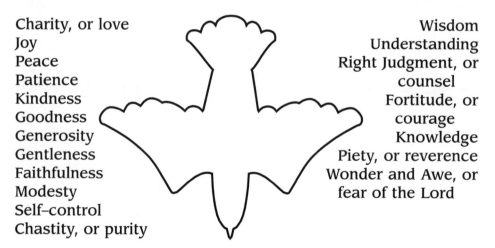

Fruits of the Holy Spirit	Gifts of the Holy Spirit
Charity, or love	Wisdom
Joy	Understanding
Peace	Right Judgment, or counsel
Patience	Fortitude, or courage
Kindness	Knowledge
Goodness	Piety, or reverence
Generosity	Wonder and Awe, or fear of the Lord
Gentleness	
Faithfulness	
Modesty	
Self–control	
Chastity, or purity	

These are handy lists to learn!

Change takes time. As we grow up, we will grow in faith. As we grow old, we will grow in faith. The Holy Spirit will guide us and teach us. The BIG Church will support us. All we need is a commitment to love and follow Jesus!

What will the path be like? Start from the inside. First cross out all the P's. Then write the words in the lines below.

```
U H C P E H T P P O T P G
R                       N
C   I S N I P E H T P   O
H D                 M   L
P E   Y L E R U   O     E
P P P       S   R       B
T O W   S   P   F   P
H U E   L   Y   P   E
A T P   O W L   G       W
T P A           N       P
P P R E P S T R O       P
J F                     Y
E   U L L Y P P F I R M L
S
U S P B R I N G S P A B O U T
```

_____

_____

_____

_____

Confirmation is our commitment to love and follow Jesus.

Celebrate With Jesus

Eucharist—the Example

Jesus celebrated the first Eucharist at his Last Supper.

On the night before he died, Jesus and his disciples shared the Passover meal. During the meal, Jesus took bread and gave thanks. He broke the bread and gave it to his followers. Then he said, "This is my body which is given for you. Do this in memory of me."

Jesus did the same thing with the wine. He took the cup and said, "This cup is the new covenant in my blood. It will be shed for you." (See Luke 22:14-20.)

After Jesus returned to heaven, his disciples continued to celebrate the Eucharist. They recognized Jesus in the breaking of the bread. The Holy Spirit helped them love and serve one another.

When we celebrate Eucharist, we celebrate with Jesus. He is the example that we follow. We are his disciples. We share his special meal. And we do it in memory of him.

Here are some highlights of our celebration.
- We praise God.
- We pray about our thoughts, words, and actions. We seek forgiveness from God and from one another.
- We hear sacred stories from the Bible. The priest tells us what they mean for our lives.
- The priest consecrates the bread and wine, which become the Body and Blood of Jesus.
- We receive Jesus in the Eucharist.

Eucharist is a BIG celebration. It is so BIG that we celebrate it every Sunday. Then Jesus' example will guide us during the week. Our celebration is called the Mass. We gather together. We sing and pray. We receive Jesus in the Eucharist.

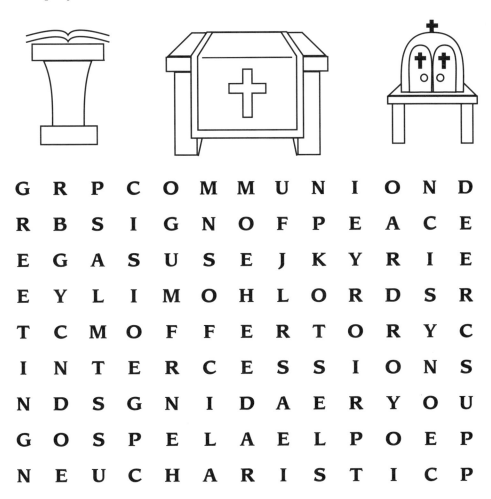

G	R	P	C	O	M	M	U	N	I	O	N	D
R	B	S	I	G	N	O	F	P	E	A	C	E
E	G	A	S	U	S	E	J	K	Y	R	I	E
E	Y	L	I	M	O	H	L	O	R	D	S	R
T	C	M	O	F	F	E	R	T	O	R	Y	C
I	N	T	E	R	C	E	S	S	I	O	N	S
N	D	S	G	N	I	D	A	E	R	Y	O	U
G	O	S	P	E	L	A	E	L	P	O	E	P
N	E	U	C	H	A	R	I	S	T	I	C	P

Look for these prayers in the puzzle above. Look for them in your Mass book, too. Then listen for them at Mass!

Greeting
Kyrie
Gloria
Readings
Psalm

Gospel
Homily
Creed
Intercessions
Offertory

Eucharistic (Prayer)
Lord's (Prayer)
Sign of Peace
Communion

Celebrate With Jesus

We are disciples of Jesus. Imagine what that means! We are his friends. We gather at his table. And we share his special meal. But Jesus gives us much more than bread and wine.

Jesus' gift is like the word below—we don't see it, but we know it's there. What is this gift called? Lay a pencil along the dotted lines. Now you can see it!

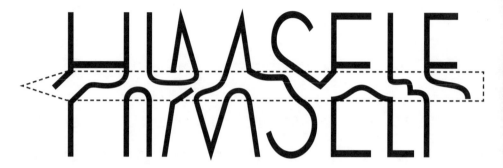

Did you know that Jesus' *present* is his *presence*? Decide which word-pair below completes each of these sentences.

1. Jesus is present in the word of God. We hear sacred stories from the Bible. We _____ and _____ about Jesus.

2. Jesus is present in the church community. We care for one another. We _____ and _____ in his name.

3. Jesus is present in the Eucharist. We are nourished.
We _____ and _____ like Jesus.

Word-Pairs
believe and become • gather and share • listen and learn

When we celebrate Eucharist, something changes. The bread and wine change to Jesus himself. And we change, too. Together, we become the "Body of Christ." We become more and more like Jesus. That is God's desire for all of us.

Change the scrambled words in the sentences below.
Then see how we become the "Body of Christ."

Our **YEES** _____ will see clearly.

Our **RESA** _____ will listen carefully.

Our **SOMUTH** _____ will speak honestly.

Our **RAMS** _____ will hug tenderly.

Our **DNAHS** _____ will help generously.

Our **GELS** _____ will walk peacefully.

Our **TEEF** _____ will follow Jesus closely.

Our **DNIMS** _____ will think wisely.

Our **THEARS** _____ will love joyfully.

Word List

arms	feet	legs
ears	hands	minds
eyes	hearts	mouths

Eucharist is our most excellent example for following Jesus!

Celebrate With Jesus

Reconciliation—a Return

Jesus celebrated Reconciliation. He welcomed sinful people the same way God does.

Zacchaeus needed God's love. He was a dishonest tax collector. So he had lots of money! One day, he climbed a tree to see Jesus. Jesus saw him there. He told Zacchaeus he would stay at his house.

The people mumbled. They wondered why Jesus went to a sinner's house! But Jesus knew why. And Zacchaeus knew why—he needed God's love.

Later that day, Zacchaeus promised to make up for his sins. Jesus said, "Today you and your family have been saved. The Son of Man came to look for and to save people who are lost." (See Luke 19:1-10.)

When we celebrate Reconciliation, we celebrate with Jesus. He welcomes us and forgives us. He is happy when we return to God's love.

Here are some highlights of our celebration.
- We pray about our thoughts, words, and actions.
- We listen to sacred stories from the Bible.
- We tell the priest about the times we did not show love. These are called "sins." They separate us from God and from one another.
- The priest suggests ways to make up for our sins.
- We say a prayer called an "act of contrition."
- The priest says a prayer called "absolution."
- We give thanks to God.

Sometimes we celebrate Reconciliation in a small room. It is called a "reconciliation room." Symbols of God's love are placed inside. Sometimes we gather together in the worship space. We celebrate our return to one another, too.

Look in this reconciliation room. Use two colors. Lightly make a checker pattern. Read the words of each color.

We	The	pray
✝ door	with	to
the	God's	priest.
♡ love	God	🕯 is
forgives	📖 open	our
to	sins.	you!

Look for the reconciliation room in your church.

19

celebrate With Jesus

God forgives us. Imagine what that means! We can be honest. We can learn from our mistakes. And we can keep on trying. God's loving hug wraps us in another invisible gift.

God's gift is like the word below—we don't see it, but we know it's there. What is this gift called? Lay a pencil along the dotted lines. Now you can see it!

This gift is always ready for us. We can prepare to receive it! All we need to do is stop and think and pray. Try it today. Then do it every day! Use these questions.

For what am I thankful?

For what am I sorry?

What did I do well?

Sometimes we forget to follow Jesus. We make choices that lead us away from him. Then we feel lost! But Jesus always loves us. He always welcomes us. At Reconciliation, we celebrate our return to his love.

Find your way back to Jesus. When you are done, celebrate!

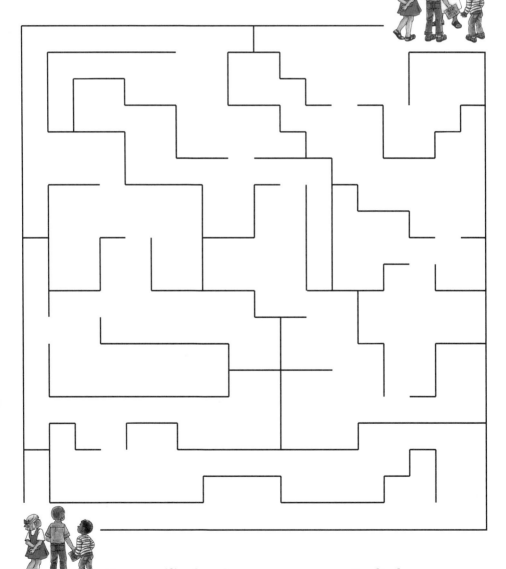

Reconciliation is our return to God's love.

Celebrate With Jesus

Anointing of the Sick—
Acceptance and Strength

Jesus celebrated healing. He cured people who had many different illnesses. He accepted them as they were. And he gave them strength to recover.

One day, Jesus was going to Jerusalem. Ten people watched for him. They had a disease called leprosy. People thought it was very contagious!

The ten lepers stayed far away from Jesus. They yelled, "Jesus, Master, have pity on us!" Jesus told them to go to the temple. On their way, they were cured!

One of them returned. He praised God and thanked Jesus. Jesus wondered about the other nine. But then he told that one, "Your faith has made you well." (See Luke 17:11-19.)

When we celebrate Anointing of the Sick, we celebrate with Jesus. He accepts us as we are, even when we are sick. He heals us in ways we do not see. Then we have new strength to live in God's love.

Here are some highlights of our celebration.
- We pray about our thoughts, words, and actions.
- We listen to sacred stories from the Bible.
- We pray for all people who are sick.
- The priest prays for the sick persons who are present. He lays his hands on their heads.
- The priest anoints their foreheads and hands with blessed oil.
- We pray the Lord's Prayer.

When we celebrate Anointing of the Sick, we celebrate God's gift of healing. Sometimes, our bodies get sick. Our hearts get sad. And our souls get stuck. We depend on God. Our faith makes us whole.

We depend on one another, too. Do you see emptiness in the words below? Fill them with **h**, **u**, **g**, *or* **s**.

Hugs help u___ stay healt___y. T___ey can red___ce stre___s and loneline___s. T___ey can ___ive u___ ener___y, too.

Hugs are whole___ome. T___ey are made from nat___ral in___redient___, like care and concern. **Hugs** do not need pre___ervative___. T___ey do not ___poil! **Hugs** are nat___rally ___weet. T___ey do not cau___e cavitie___.

Hugs ___ive u___ a ___ood do___e of love. T___ey do not have side effect___. B___t be caref___l. T___ey can be very conta___iou___!

**Do you see emptiness in the people you know?
Fill them with hugs!**

celebrate With Jesus

Matrimony—a Miracle

Jesus celebrated at a wedding. It was in the village of Cana. He attended it with his mother, Mary, and with his disciples.

During the celebration, the hosts ran out of wine. Mary told Jesus about it. She wanted him to help. But Jesus said he wasn't ready yet. He wasn't ready to be known as God's Son.

Mary talked to the servants anyway. She told them to do whatever Jesus told them to do.

Jesus told the servants to fill six huge jars with water. Then he told them to take some of the water to the head waiter. By that time, the water had turned into wine! The waiter did not know where it came from. But he told the bridegroom that the new wine was much better than the old! (See John 2:1-11.)

Jesus celebrated marriage. In fact, he performed his first miracle at this wedding! When we celebrate marriage—the sacrament we call Matrimony—we celebrate with Jesus. We celebrate the miraculous love that exists between a married couple.

Either a priest or deacon can witness a marriage. Here are some highlights of our celebration.

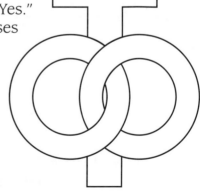

- We listen to sacred stories from the Bible.
- The priest or deacon asks the bride and groom three key questions about Christian marriage. They answer "Yes."
- The bride and groom make promises to each other.
- They exchange rings.
- The priest or deacon introduces the new couple.

When we celebrate marriage, we celebrate God's gift of love. The couple promises to share it with each other. God's love will help them honor and care for each other. It will help them honor and care for their families, too.

What makes marriage miraculous? Follow the arrows to find a message. Write the letters in the blanks below.

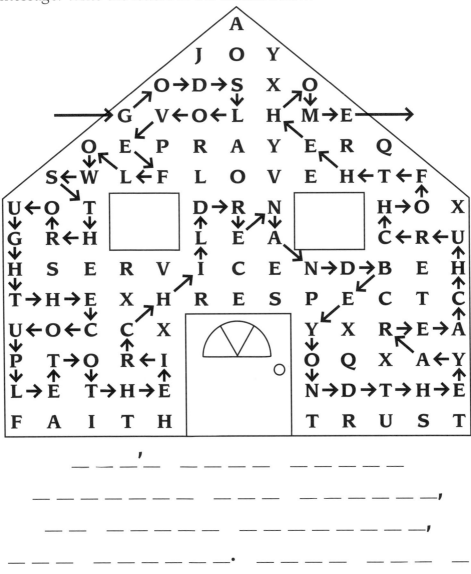

_ _ _ ' _ _ _ _ _ _ _ _ _

_ _ _ _ _ _ _ _ _ _ _ _ _ _ _ _ —'

_ _ _ _ _ _ _ _ _ _ _ _ _ _ —'

_ _ _ _ _ _ _ _ _ . _ _ _ _ _ _ _ _

"_ _ _ _ _ _ _ _ _ _ _ _ _ _ _ _ _ _ _ ."

Celebrate With Jesus

Holy Orders—
Hearing and Obeying

Jesus had a mission: He wanted to show God's love to all people. He asked some fishermen to help. He said, "Come with me! I will teach you to catch people instead of fish." (See Matthew 4:18-19.)

After the resurrection, Jesus wanted his followers to continue his mission. He said,

> Go to the people of all nations and make them my disciples. Baptize them in the name of the Father, the Son, and the Holy Spirit, and teach them to do everything I have told you. I will be with you always, even until the end of time. (See Matthew 28:18-20.)

Jesus called on helpers to continue his mission. They heard his call and they obeyed. When we celebrate Holy Orders, we celebrate with Jesus. He calls on new men to help him. They hear his call, and they obey. This is their vocation.

The bishop confers Holy Orders on priests and deacons. Here are some highlights of the Holy Orders' celebration for a priest.
- We listen to sacred stories from the Bible.
- The bishop asks the candidates four key questions about the work of a priest. They answer "Yes."
- The bishop places his hands on the candidates' heads. He consecrates them with prayer.
- The candidates receive their vestments. Their hands are anointed with the oil of chrism.
- We celebrate the Eucharist.

When we celebrate Holy Orders, we celebrate God's gift of vocations. "Vocation" means "call." The new priests or deacons will share the Good News. They will care for God's people. And they will celebrate the sacraments!

Priests wear special clothes to celebrate sacraments. They are called "vestments." Color these Mass vestments with joyful colors!

We all have vocations. God gives us gifts to serve one another. Listen when you pray. Is Jesus calling you?

Celebrate With Jesus

We are **1**-_____. When we celebrate our faith, we celebrate with Jesus. Here are the celebrations.

Baptism is the beginning. God's gift is "opened" for us. This gift is **2** (across)-_____. It is a share of God's divine life and **2** (down)-_____.

Confirmation is our commitment to love and follow Jesus. The Holy Spirit inspires us with the **3**-_____ of love. As we grow in faith, we use our unique talents to **4**-_____ God.

Eucharist is the example for following Jesus. He is **5** (across)-_____ in many ways: He is present in the **5** (down)-_____ because we gather in his name. He is present in the **6**-_____ of God because we hear Bible stories about him. And he is present in the **7**-_____ and wine.

Sometimes we forget to follow Jesus. **Reconciliation** is our return to his love. He gives us forgiveness and **8**-_____.

When we receive **Anointing of the Sick**, we receive God's gift of **9**-_____. God heals us in ways we do not see.

Marriage is miraculous, because God's **10**-_____ flows between the husband and wife. It helps them **11**-_____ for each other and their children.

Holy Orders is hearing and obeying God's call to become a priest or deacon. This call is a unique **12**-_____.

Celebration Crosswords

bread	grace	present
care	healing	serve
children of God	love	vocation
energy	mercy	word
goodness	people	

We celebrate all this, and even more....

Celebrate With Jesus

God's love is amazing! You have just learned about seven celebrations of faith. These are called "sacraments." Sacred objects remind us that God is always with us. Always! These are called "sacramentals."

Complete these pictures of sacramentals. Remember, God is present with complete love!

Palms proclaim "Hosanna!"

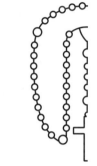

Rosaries represent Mary's love.

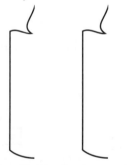

Candles light the way of Christ.

Bibles tell the word of God.

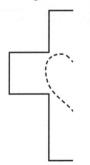

Crosses carry Jesus' love.

Holy water sprinkles blessings.

**What sacramentals are in your church?
Your home? Your car?**

God is present in the sacraments. God is present in our daily activities. And God is always ready to give us grace. Always! All we need to do is notice the sacred moments. This is called "sacramental living."

How do you make space for grace? Follow the code for ideas.

Code

⌐⊥ = A	= E	= I	= N	= S
= B	= F	= K	= O	= T
= C	= G	= L	= P	= W
= D	= H	= M	= R	= Y

31

Activity Answers

Page 4
stories, rituals, symbols, people, gifts

Page 7
See! You are also a beloved child of God!

Page 9
Your light will shine as bright as mine.
Follow me!

Page 11
You are sealed. The Holy Spirit will inspire
you with the energy of love.

Page 13
Slowly, surely we are strong from the inside
out. Fully, firmly we belong to the Church
that Jesus brings about.

Page 15

Page 16: HIMSELF
1. listen and learn
2. gather and share
3. believe and become

Page 17
eyes; ears; mouths; arms; hands; legs; feet;
minds; hearts

Page 19
We pray with the priest. God forgives our
sins. The door to God's love is open to you.

Page 21

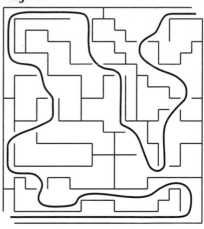

Page 23
Hugs help us stay healthy. They can
reduce stress and loneliness. They can
give us energy, too.

Hugs are wholesome. They are made
from natural ingredients, like care and
concern. Hugs do not need preservatives.
They do not spoil! Hugs are naturally
sweet. They do not cause cavities.

Hugs give us a good dose of love.
They do not have side effects. But be
careful. They can be very contagious!

Page 25
God's love flows through the couple, to
their children, and beyond. They are a
"church of the home."

Page 28-29
1-children of God   2-grace; goodness
3-energy   4-serve   5-present; people
6-word   7-bread   8-mercy   9-healing
10-love   11-care   12-vocation

Page 31
Treat all of creation
   with kindness and care.
Each day is a blessing
   so take time for prayer.